EMPOWERMENT

Understanding the Theory Behind Empowerment

Jimmy D. Bayes

DUNAMIS PUBLICATIONS

EMPOWERMENT: UNDERSTANDING THE THEORY BEHIND EMPOWERMENT

Copyright © 2015 Dunamis Publications
A service of Dunamis Empowerment Foundation
1716 Briarcrest Flr3
Bryan, TX 77802

ISBN: 0996582401
ISBN-13: 978-0-9965824-0-7

Printed in the United States

Communication or requests to the author should be addressed electronically to dunamisempower@gmail.com or by mail to Dr. J. D. Bayes, c/o Dunamis Empowerment Foundation, 1716 Briarcrest Flr 3, Bryan, TX 77802.

This publication is designed to provide accurate and authoritative information in regard to the subject matter covered. It is provided with the understanding that the author is not responsible for the results that may occur in applying the following information.

MISSION OF

DUNAMIS EMPOWERMENT FOUNDATION

Dunamis Empowerment Foundation ("Dunamis") exists to promote the social, structural, psychological, and divine empowerment of individuals and organizations through various means of communication including but not limited to books, articles, publications, seminars, social media, speaking engagements, and by networking with other empowering organizations.

DUNAMIS PUBLICATIONS

Dunamis Publications is a service of the Dunamis Empowerment Foundation that helps empower groups and individuals by helping to publish works they have written. The goal of Dunamis Publications is to help publish and market publications. Visit us at www.dunamisempower.org to find out more about our publishing process.

Please look for other Dunamis Publications or if you would like to have more information about how you can publish your book, contact us through our website.

THANK YOU FOR YOUR SUPPORT

Dunamis Empowerment Foundation was established in 2014 to address people's feelings of powerlessness by promoting social, structural, psychological, and divine empowerment. Your support will directly empower many individuals and groups that desire to empower others so they can gain the control of their lives and futures. Empowering individuals will ultimately empower communities. Dunamis' motto and goal is to *Empower People to Empower People*. Please sign up for our periodic update by going to www.dunamisempower.org and registering.

CONTENTS

1
EMPOWERMENT
IN
ORGANIZATIONS

To understand empowerment in society, a look at how empowerment has developed in organizational literature is helpful. The concepts that apply to organizations can also apply to groups and individuals. More than 70% of organizations surveyed have adopted some sort of empowerment practice in at least a portion of their workforce. However, empowerment is not understood the same from organization to organization. Many concepts are often used in organizational literature as acts of empowerment. Some of these concepts are: delegation of authority, employee motivation, self-efficacy, job enrichment, employee ownership, employee autonomy, self-determination, self-management, self-control, self-influence, high-involvement, and participation in decision making and planning. With this ambiguity comes much debate over the concept of empowerment.

Serious study concerning organizational empowerment began in the late 80's and continues today. Interestingly, empowerment as an organizational concept has had some difficulty gaining wide support. In 1998, organizational expert, Chris Argyris wrote that despite all of the talk, empowerment is still mostly an illusion. He further insisted that managers like empowerment in theory but have less trust in it than the traditional "command-and-control model," and he feels that employees are often ambivalent about empowerment. L. Landes was more critical towards empowerment stating that employee empowerment is a misguided notion that is mostly a myth in many organizations. He explained by saying that, ultimately, management must take responsibility for control in the organization and execute the master plan. He writes that employees need to be "equipped," not empowered. Many organizations have all but ignored empowerment because of the lack of a universally accepted concept or definition of empowerment. While some organizations struggle with how and how much to empower their employees, Joanne Ciulla warns of bogus empowerment. Bogus empowerment is when employees are told that they have been empowered, but they know that they are not. An example is when a company announces that they are going to empower their employees by letting them choose the color scheme of the new offices. Selecting color schemes does not substantially increase the power one needs to control their jobs. Effective empowerment decisions should make a real difference in the experience of the employees. Empowerment should substantially impact the ability of the individual to gain more control over his job, life, and future.

In spite of these criticisms (or maybe because of them), organizational researchers have put forth several empowerment theories and models. There is now a body of research that gives legitimacy to their theories. There are three primary avenues of when examining empowerment:

1. Critical social view
2. Structural view
3. Psychological view

Social empowerment is not often considered in organizational settings, but it is popular among groups that feel disenfranchised or have feelings of powerlessness such as women's groups, gay and lesbian groups, ethnic groups and other social groups. Social empowerment focuses on gaining social status, equal treatment and participation in decision making to gain more control over their life and destiny. Structural and psychological empowerment has gained much support in many organizations and is aimed at helping members gain access to resources and building confidence to accomplish their tasks. All three kinds of empowerment take place in every aspect of life. It is our belief that individuals can experience feelings of powerlessness in all three of the areas.

There is another type of empowerment that is not often talked about outside Christian circles. I am referring to spiritual empowerment. This type of empowerment, however, has not been well defined. Chapter four introduces the concept of what I refer to as divine empowerment. Divine or spiritual empowerment is introduced here, but there will be a fuller description of this empowerment model in another publication. An understanding of all aspects of powerlessness, the causes of powerlessness, and methods to address these needs will help people and organizations be more efficient in empowering others.

Empowering Individuals

I am asked how an individual can empower another individual. Most organizations that empower people, do so in specific ways. Often, a person or group of people identify a particular need and make efforts to meet that need. For example, foster kids that have been aged out of the foster care system often lack the resources or information they require to make good life choices, so an organization forms mentoring programs to empower these foster kids by giving them access to resources and information. Organizations have started giving micro-loans to women in India to empower them to start small businesses so that they can escape poverty and gain control of their lives. A lady in New York started a program that gets inner city youth involved in competitive rowing empowering them by teaching them discipline, team work, and participation, and helping them to gain access to opportunities which boosts their confidence. Most organizations offering some type of empowerment either take the empowerment to the public or individuals come to the organization for their services. All of these empowering efforts are important.

The Dunamis method offers an alternative by first listening to the person, identifying their areas of powerlessness as social, structural, psychological, or spiritual and then empowering them according to these feelings of powerlessness. This method reduces the chances of someone using many resources and still being left with the feeling that they have little control over their lives. Lacking access to resources is probably the easiest cause of powerlessness to identify. However, powerlessness caused by the lack of resources is often accompanied by feelings of powerlessness. Many times unless these feelings are addressed having access to more resources may not lead to desired feelings of empowerment. These other sources of powerlessness should be addressed first or at least in conjunction with the lack of resources.

This book briefly reviews the important concepts that have contributed to the understanding of organizational empowerment and is not intended to be a comprehensive description of empowerment outside of an organizational context. We do not intend to criticize any organization or their empowerment efforts as any organization whose mission is to empower others should be commended. The mission of the Dunamis Empowerment Foundation is to bring awareness to an individual's and organizations full empowerment potential. By "full empowerment potential" we are referring to the consideration of social, structural, psychological, and divine dimensions of empowerment. These dimensions have been combined into an integrated model called the Empower4 or E4 model. A book on this model will be released sometime in the next year.

2
SOCIAL EMPOWERMENT

Many people feel that they have been marginalized and have been treated unfairly by society. Usually these individuals have identified with a social group that has been perceived as being treated unequally or unfairly. This dynamic is commonly a shared experience that comes from membership in a social group. There are many such groups based on some common aspect such as gender, youth, ethnicity, sexual preference, physical or mental handicap, place of residence, vocation, educational level, age, etc. However, feelings of social injustice and unfair treatment can also happen to individuals outside of a specific social group. The critical social theory explains many of the commonalities that disenfranchised groups' experience.

Some researchers have applied the critical social theory to empowerment. Critical social theory can be traced back to the Frankfurt School in Germany. Critical social theory was inspired by Marxist philosophy. Critical social theory assumes three things.

1. Certain social groups are in a subordinate position

2. Institutions are often the bastions of unequal distribution of power and privilege
3. Empowerment is equal to liberation

The use of critical social theory for research is based on the assumption that people are capable of self-reflection and that all people have a basic need to act independently. Critical social empowerment is aimed specifically at a dimension of power where the unseen institutional power shapes the ideas and values of the individual and the organization. Social activists and proponents of critical social theory such as Paulo Freire believe that social conditions distort the individual's self-perception and that insights from the critical social theory will enable people to see their conditions for what they are and find ways of changing them to become free. For these individuals, education is the key to empowerment. The premise of Freire's work is that liberating and empowering education is a process that involves listening, dialogue, critical reflection, and reflective action. Engagement between teacher and pupil reveals powerless situations and together they can formulate a social action agenda. Thus, the fresh awareness of their situation inspires belief in the capacity to change their situation. Because the state of the oppressed or unempowered varies, the empowerment agenda is different depending upon the condition and the situation of the subordinate individual or group.

Although it is limited, research shows some validity of critical social empowerment in organizations. In a qualitative study, it was found that teaching critical social theory was an important empowerment practice in the nursing profession. Nursing in the United Kingdom has been found to be an oppressed group because of gender bias, occupational bias, and class inequality. In two focus groups, it was found that their nurses did not feel empowered, they lacked confidence, and they had low self-esteem. The researcher found the focus groups conceptualized empowerment in terms of freedom. They desired the freedom to make decisions with authority and to have choices that affected their jobs and lives. In another study, it was found that critical social empowerment shows that to reach their greatest potential in contributing to the organization, nurses should be empowered by having an equal voice in decision-making with the doctors and administrators.

Critical social empowerment is still in the early stages of development and a comprehensive social empowerment model has not been developed. One study, however, has developed a critical social model of empowerment for youth that may apply to larger groups. This model has six aspects:

1. A safe and supportive environment
2. Meaningful participation
3. Shared power
4. Individual and community level orientation
5. Sociopolitical change goals
6. Critical reflection

These six aspects are consistent with other research in critical social empowerment and should provide the basis for a social empowerment model. As currently understood, social awareness is the starting point in critical social empowerment and seems to lay the blame for feelings of powerlessness on social inequality. While this may be good on a group level, an individual in American society is not held captive by their social status. Success stories are common where an individual overcomes drastic circumstances to achieve their dreams of success. In the background of each of these success stories are usually organizations or individuals helping empower them toward success. We should develop the ability to identify a person's feelings of powerlessness that results from identifying with a particular social group experiencing some level of social injustice. With the right resources, good support, and encouragement, social issues become less an obstacle to an individual's success. Additional social empowerment models will likely be developed as critical social empowerment research continues.

3
STRUCTURAL EMPOWERMENT

Often feeling of powerlessness come from lack of resources (mainly money) or not having the ability, knowledge, skills, or experience needed to provide the kind of lifestyle one would hope to live. This sense of powerlessness is addressed by the second, and probably the most popular view of empowerment: structural empowerment. This model of empowerment (developed for use in organizations) comes from the book, *Men and Women of the Corporation,* by Rosabeth Moss Kanter and her definition of power. She defines power as access to organizational structures in the work environment through lines of communication, support, information, and resources that offers workers the opportunities to share in decision-making processes, assist in control of resources, and to grow into their jobs. For Kanter, empowerment evolves from two kind of capacities:

1. Having access to resources, information, and support necessary to carry out a task
2. Having the ability to get cooperation in doing what is necessary

These capacities are provided by informal and formal power in the workplace. The basic ideas behind Kanter's model is in the power and opportunity structures created by the organization and not in the individual's abilities. Structural empowerment consists of four components:

1. Information
2. Resources
3. Opportunities
4. Support

Information means having the knowledge of organizational decisions, policies, goals as well as the data, technical knowledge, and expertise required to be effective. Having this information gives the individual a sense of purpose and meaning for employees and enhances their ability to make judgements and influence organizational decisions.

Resources refers to the capacity of the individual to access the materials, funds, supplies, time, and equipment required to accomplish organizational goals.

Opportunities are for mobility and growth that entail having access to challenges, rewards, and professional development experiences that increases knowledge, skills, and influence. Opportunities may be provided through participation on committees, task forces, and interdepartmental work groups that provide opportunities to work with individuals in other areas of the organization.

Support includes feedback and guidance from superiors, peers, and subordinates. Support may also consist of emotional support, helpful advice, and personal assistance.

Structural empowerment is relational and describes the perceived power or control that a leader has over others. Power over others come from one or more of the following sources:

1. The office or position held (position power or legitimate power). This power has control over rewards and punishments.
2. Personal characteristics (referent power)
3. The expertise of the person (expert power)
4. Access to specialized knowledge (informational power)

Structural empowerment was developed by Kanter and others for use in organizations, but the principles apply to anyone who is powerless regardless of context. Organizations empower their employees so that they can accomplish company goals and outside the organizational context, people need empowered by gaining access to resources to have control of their lives and futures.

Jay Conger and Rabindra Kanungo believe that structural empowerment has led organizations to focus on the source of power and to the conditions that promote these sources of power and ultimately led to the development of strategies to distribute resources in efforts to increase power for employees. Kanter's research showed how many women lacked certain "power tools" (information, resources, opportunity, and support). Employees at low levels of hierarchy can be empowered if they have access to these power tools. The essence of structural empowerment is the idea of sharing power between superiors and subordinates with the goal of having those at lower levels eventually share in decision-making. In spite of gaining many of these power tools, many still feel unempowered and others that lack these tools can feel and act in empowered ways. The reason that some feel empowered and others do not—regardless of their possession of power tools—indicates that giving information, resources, opportunities, and support is not enough for some people to have the sense of empowerment. This fact caused some researchers to look for psychological factors of empowerment.

4
PSYCHOLOGICAL EMPOWERMENT

It has been determined that providing the power tools of structural empowerment does not necessarily lead to feelings of empowerment. These tools are only one variable in the empowerment process. Structural empowerment is defined in terms of providing structure and support. Addressing the psychological aspect of empowerment, Jay Conger and Rabindra Kanungo have offered an alternate definition of empowerment:

> *Empowerment is defined as a process of enhancing feelings of self-efficacy among organizational members through identification of conditions that foster powerlessness and through their removal by both formal organizational practices and informal techniques of providing efficacy information.*

This concept of empowerment is motivational and is based upon two types of expectancy:

1. That their efforts will result in a desired level of performance
2. That their performance will produce desired results

The first expectancy is known as self-efficacy and the second is known as outcome expectation. (Self-efficacy is the ability to produce a desired or intended result.) When individuals are empowered, their personal efficacy and expectations are strengthened. Thus, empowerment refers to a process where an individual's belief in one's self-efficacy is enhanced and to empower means either to strengthen this belief or to weaken one's belief in personal powerlessness.

Psychological empowerment has also been conceptualized in terms of mental or physical tasks that determine motivation. It is argued that empowerment is multifaceted and its essence cannot be explained by a single concept. Thus, this psychologically-oriented empowerment can be defined as the increased motivation to accomplish tasks. This motivation is determined by how the individual relates to his work role. A person thinks about his job role in four ways:

1. Impact
2. Competence
3. Meaningfulness
4. Self-determination

Impact is the degree to which an individual can influence strategic, administrative, or operating outcomes at work; **competence** (self-efficacy) is the individual's belief in their own capability to perform tasks with skill; **meaning** is the value of a work goal or purpose; **self-determination** is an individual's sense of having choice in initiating and regulating actions.

To distinguish between structural empowerment and psychological empowerment, it has been said that structural empowerment is the perception of the presence or absence of empowering conditions in the workplace and that psychological empowerment is the employee's psychological interpretation or relation to these conditions. Psychological empowerment represents a reaction of employees to structural empowerment. Many have viewed empowerment as the change in an individual's internal motivation as a result of changes to structure, policies, or practices. This assumes the presence of both psychological and structural empowerment. It begs the question whether one can empower in one aspect and not the other.

There seems to be a consensus that structural empowerment is a management technique used to improve outcomes and is built upon the notion that superiors distribute power, responsibility, and information to others. Structural empowerment is the application of management practices and psychological empowerment is how these applications are understood. Psychological empowerment and structural empowerment are two distinct forms of empowerment but the best method of empowerment is integrating the two. I suggest that elements of social empowerment and divine empowerment (next section) should also be considered in any comprehensive holistic empowerment model. However, there has not been a fully integrated model of empowerment developed (until now).

5
DIVINE
EMPOWERMENT

A 2011 Gallup poll found that 9 of every 10 people in America still believe in God. A Pew research report says that almost 93% of Americans consider themselves Christian and 6% are of another faith and only 2.4% of Americans call themselves atheist. Interestingly, 24% of the people that call themselves atheist also consider themselves to be spiritual. The point is that the vast majority of Americans are religious or spiritual at their core. However, most spirituality—especially Christianity—has been barred from most of our organizations.

The news is not all bad for those wanting to make their spiritual life an integral part of their lives and not just their personal life. Feature articles in *Newsweek, Time, Fortune,* and *Business Week* have highlighted the growing acceptance of spirituality in corporate America. Issues regarding workplace spirituality have been receiving increased attention in organizational sciences and there has been a move toward spirituality in leadership studies. Influenced by the interest in spirituality in the workplace, Louis Fry has developed a theory of spiritual leadership for organizations that has been gaining acceptance. Fry defines spiritual leadership as the values, attitudes, and behaviors that are necessary to internally motivate one's self and others so they have a sense of spiritual well-being through calling and membership. In practical application, spiritual leadership is a motivational model that incorporates vision, hope/faith, altruistic love, and theories of workplace spirituality and well-being. The ultimate purpose of spiritual leadership is injecting vision and values across all levels of the organization and fostering high levels of commitment and productivity. Spiritual leadership is accomplished by creating a vision where leaders and followers experience a sense of calling where life has meaning and makes a difference and by establishing a social culture based on the values of altruistic love where the leaders and followers have a sense of membership, feel understood and appreciated, and have genuine care, concern, and appreciation for self and others.

Organizations are starting to realize that because most of their members have an important spiritual component to their lives this spiritual aspect should be addressed. This does not mean the organizations sponsor spiritual aspects, but they are starting to acknowledge and support this area of their members lives. A special issue of *The Leadership Quarterly* on the subject of workplace spirituality and spiritual leadership revealed three themes required for workplace spirituality as a concept:

1. An inner life that nourishes and is nourished by...
2. ...a calling or transcendence of self within the context of...
3. ...community based on values of altruistic love.

This definition of spirituality is nonreligious, and religion has been virtually disregarded in the study of spirituality in the workplace. The likely reasons for this snub is the possibility of division, religious exclusivity, arrogance, zealotry, offense, and the potential for a decrease in morale, employee well-being, and organizational goals. This spirituality, however acknowledges the presence of a higher-power instead of a specific deity. This higher-power may or may not be centered in a religious context. This nonreligious spirituality is broader than any organized religion with tenets, doctrines, and dogma. This nonreligious spirituality has at least four characteristics:

1. A belief in a higher power or higher meaning to life
2. Conscious attempts to understand and connect with a higher power or meaning
3. The transcendence of self
4. The connectedness to others

Proponents of this spirituality believe that it is necessary for religion, but religion is not necessary for this spirituality. Supporters of this type of spirituality do not speak much about spiritual empowerment, but it can be assumed that a person would be "spiritually empowered" as they experience each of the four characteristics listed above.

Divergent Views of Spiritual Empowerment

In this section I outlined the need for organizations to support their member's spiritual lives. If promoting a belief in God (or higher power), helping people connect with God, helping the person look beyond themselves, and helping people connect with others is called spiritual empowerment, then organizations should add spiritual empowerment to their empowering efforts.

Since I have started promoting the spiritual aspect of empowerment, I have had two distinct reactions from Christian groups and secular organizations. On the one hand, many secular organizations seem to lose interest when I begin talking about spiritual empowerment even after I explain that the majority of Americans believe in God and have a spiritual core. On the other hand, Christians that I have talked with seem to think that these aspects of empowerment are not Christian enough as presented here. They seem to imply that people only need to be empowered spiritually. They also feel that spiritual empowerment as outlined should be grounded firmly in scripture. I agree. My doctoral thesis developed a model of divine empowerment developed from a comprehensive examination of Ephesians 4:1-16. (A publication on this model of divine empowerment is to be published soon.) Christian groups and secular organizations should find areas wherein they can agree and focus on them. We have been told for too many years that God and religion have no place in society outside of our churches and homes. I must disagree respectfully. An individual's spirituality should not be ignored. Being spiritually empowered will have profound effects upon the lives of everyone and their organizations would ultimately benefit from their empowerment.

6
THE NEED FOR AN INTEGRATED MODEL OF EMPOWERMENT

Seldom a day goes by that I don't hear or read of a person empowering someone or being empowered. Empowerment is everywhere and there are many ways to empower. Since beginning the study of empowerment, I have taken note every time I hear "empowerment." In each instance where a person or group says they empower others, I examine it to determine what kind of empowerment they offer. Without fail I can identify it as either social, structural, psychological, spiritual or a combination of these. Two questions come to mind when I hear a person or organization describe the manner in which they empower.

1. Are they aware of what kind of empowerment they are providing?
2. Are they aware of their full empowerment potential?

The previous chapters have outlined the various ways that people and organizations have approached empowerment. Organizations have had various levels of success empowering others. There has long been a need for the development of an integrated empowerment model that includes all four aspects of empowerment. My doctoral research was developing a model of divine empowerment from the New Testament. (I use the term divine empowerment to distinguish it from spiritual empowerment as outlined in the previous chapter.) The goal of my doctoral research was to develop a Biblical model of empowerment and to integrate that model into a holistic empowerment model that includes social, structural, psychological, and divine aspects. This book has introduced the theory behind empowerment as it is currently understood in the organizational setting. These empowering principles can and should be applied in other contexts. People with feelings of powerlessness are all around us and we have the ability to empower them. We may not see that individual achieve the success that they want, but we can help that person move forward, sometime with baby steps, sometimes with great strides. We should be able to identify areas where people feel powerless over some aspect of their life and know what kind of empowerment they need, and move them toward having more power or control in that area.

This book also states the need for a model of spiritual empowerment and the need for an integrated model of empowerment. Please go to www.dunamisempower.org and learn more about *Empower4* and look for additional empowering resources.

SOURCES

Argyris, C. (1998). Empowerment: The emperor's new clothes. Harvard Business Review, 98-105.

Ciulla, J. (2004). Leadership and the problem of bogus empowerment. In J. Ciulla (Ed.), Ethics, the heart of leadership (2nd ed., pp. 59-82). Westport, CT: PRAEGER.

Conger, J. A., & Kanungo, R. N. (1988). The empowerment process: Integrating theory and practice. Academy of Management Review, 13(3), 471-482. doi:10.2307/258093

Fry, L. W. (2003). Toward a theory of spiritual leadership. The Leadership Quarterly, 14, 693-727. doi:10.1016/j.leaqua.2003.09.001

Fry, L. W. (2005). Introduction: Toward a paradigm of spiritual leadership. The Leadership Quarterly, 16(Special Issue), 619-622. doi:10.1016/j.leaqua.2005.07.001

Fry, L. W. (2006). Spiritual leadership and organizational performance: An exploratory study. Paper presented at the Academy of Management, Atlanta, GA.

Kanter, R. M. (1993). Men and women of the corporation (Kindle ed.). New York, NY: Basic Books.

Landes, L. (1994). The myth and misdirection of employee empowerment. Training, 31(3), 116. Retrieved from http://business.highbeam.com/137618/article-1G1-15294726/myth-and-misdirection-employee-empowerment

Spreitzer, G. M. (1995). Psychological empowerment in the workplace: Dimensions, measurement and validation. Academy of Management Journal, 38(5), 1442-1465. doi:10.2307/256865

Spreitzer, G. M. (1996). Social structural characteristics of psychological empowerment. Academy of Management, 39(2), 483-504. doi:10.2307/256789

Thomas, K. W., & Velthouse, B. A. (1990). Cognitive elements of empowerment: An "interpretive" model of intrinsic task motivation. Academy of Management Review, 15(4), 666-681. doi:10.5465/AMR.1990.4310926

This book is also available in paperback and Kindle version through Amazon.com online.

DUNAMIS

EMPOWERMENT FOUNDATION

www.ingramcontent.com/pod-product-compliance
Lightning Source LLC
Chambersburg PA
CBHW060705280326
41933CB00012B/2310